Dedicated to all
Police Officers
and their families.

Be safe always.

My Aunt is a Police Officer, so what exactly does she do?

She helps people all around, people just like me and you!

Sometimes
in the
morning,
and
sometimes
in the night,

My Aunt goes to work to make sure everything is alright.

She drives a car that has flashing lights and the siren makes a loud sound.

She wears a uniform and helps keep people safe all around!

She told me we are all part
of a family that is blue,

Police Officers and their loved ones, and other Police Aunts too!

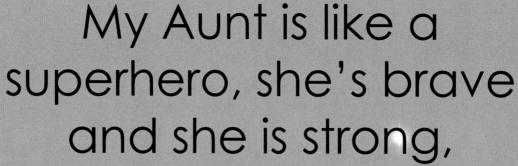

My Aunt is like a superhero, she's brave and she is strong,

She's always putting others first while working all day long

There are so many
things for her to do,

And she gets to work
with other heroes too!

Sometimes my Aunt
can't be here to play,

Because she's out there
helping save the day!

My Aunt would love to
see me all the time,

But it's hard for her to do
when she's out there
fighting crime!

When we are together,
my Aunt wants me to know

How much she really loves me,
before she has to go.

When my Aunt is working, there's one thing I know for sure

She loves me very much, and I love her even more!

Sometimes when I get into
bed after the day is through,

I dream that one day I might become a Police Officer too!

My Aunt is my hero,
each and every
day.

I love my
Police Officer
Aunt in
every single
way!

Made in the USA
Monee, IL
21 December 2022